Bloom is the perfect companion for Black women on a journey of self-care and self-awareness. This carefully designed journal is specifically tailored to support and empower Black women as they navigate their path towards personal growth and well-being. With mindfully curated prompts and evidence-based exercises, this journal provides a safe space for reflection, self-discovery, and self-expression.

Take the time to prioritize your mental, emotional, and physical health while celebrating your unique identity and experiences. Embrace this journal as a tool to cultivate self-love, resilience, and inner strength on your empowering journey.

With love,
Raven

SECTION 1   THE SEED

SECTION 2   BUDDING

SECTION 3   SPROUTING

SECTION 4   FLOWERING

SECTION 5   GROUNDING

SECTION 6   GRATITUDE

SECTION 1

THE SEED

REFLECTING ON WHO YOU ARE

The life cycle of a plant serves as a powerful metaphor for various life cycles. Just like planting a seed in the ground, where it is placed in the darkness of the earth, there are moments in our lives when we find ourselves in different circumstances.

Just as a seed needs to be enveloped in soil or a nurturing medium to initiate the germination process, we also have to face challenging situations to foster our growth. Life won't always provide you with the best conditions to facilitate growth. You may encounter obstacles, but these experiences, like the soil covering the seed, play a vital role in our personal development and the shaping of who we are.

Once planted, a miraculous, hidden process happens that takes that hard seed and cracks it open to let life out. The breaking of that seed is pivotal in the growth of an organism. Some days you will experience the breaking process and it is not going to always feel comfortable. Please know, however, that before anything can grow, it must shed its previous layer. In order to bloom, we have to allow ourselves the opportunity to break free of the shell that holds us. This freedom only comes from reflection and a deep knowing of the self.

SELF-REFLECTION:
Identifying Your Current Mindset

Reflection is the first step in understanding where you currently stand. Here are a series of questions aimed at helping you identify your mindset:

1 How do my thoughts influence my emotions and overall well-being?

2 Do I appreciate feedback and criticism, viewing them as chances to improve? Or do I become defensive and disheartened?

3 What are my beliefs about my abilities? Do I believe I can grow and change, or am I stuck with what I have?

WRITE A LETTER TO YOURSELF AT THE START OF YOUR HEALING JOURNEY, ACKNOWLEDGING YOUR GROWTH AND PROGRESS.

DATE: _____

_____

_____

_____

_____

_____

_____

_____

_____

_____

_____

_____

_____

_____

_____

_____

_____

_____

_____

_____

The Seed: Reflecting on Who You Are

WHAT DOES IT MEAN TO RECLAIM YOUR OWN NARRATIVE? HOW CAN YOU REWRITE YOUR STORY IN A WAY THAT EMPOWERS AND UPLIFTS YOU?

DATE:

The Seed: Reflecting on Who You Are

WHAT ARE THREE QUALITIES OR SKILLS YOU ADMIRE MOST IN YOURSELF? HOW CAN YOU CULTIVATE THEM FURTHER?

DATE:
_____

_____
_____
_____
_____
_____
_____
_____
_____
_____
_____
_____
_____
_____
_____
_____
_____
_____
_____
_____

The Seed: Reflecting on Who You Are

The Seed: Reflecting on Who You Are

WHEN DO YOU FEEL MOST CONNECTED TO YOUR AUTHENTIC SELF? HOW CAN YOU CULTIVATE MORE OF THOSE MOMENTS?

DATE: _____

_____
_____
_____
_____
_____
_____
_____
_____
_____
_____
_____
_____
_____
_____
_____
_____
_____
_____
_____

The Seed: Reflecting on Who You Are

The Seed: Reflecting on Who You Are

WHAT ARE THREE VALUES THAT GUIDE YOU ON YOUR HEALING JOURNEY? HOW DO THEY INFORM YOUR CHOICES AND ACTIONS?

DATE:
_____

_____
_____
_____
_____
_____
_____
_____
_____
_____
_____
_____
_____
_____
_____
_____
_____
_____
_____
_____

The Seed: Reflecting on Who You Are

The Seed: Reflecting on Who You Are

"Caring for myself is not self-indulgence, it is self-preservation, and that is an act of political warfare."
- Audre Lorde

WEEKLY CHECK-IN

THIS WEEK I'M GRATEFUL FOR

| 1 | 2 | 3 |

THINGS THAT MADE ME SMILE THIS WEEK

SOMETHING THAT INSPIRED ME THIS WEEK

CONNECTIONS THAT I MADE THIS WEEK

SOMETHING THAT WORKED WELL THIS WEEK

AREA FOR IMPROVEMENT

Set your intention for the week

WHAT DID YOUR YOUNGER SELF NEED? HOW CAN YOU POUR INTO YOUR YOUNGER SELF NOW?

DATE:

The Seed: Reflecting on Who You Are

The Seed: Reflecting on Who You Are

WRITE A LETTER TO YOUR YOUNGER SELF, OFFERING WORDS OF WISDOM AND ENCOURAGEMENT.

DATE: _____

The Seed: Reflecting on Who You Are

REFLECT ON A TIME WHEN YOU FELT TRULY SEEN AND HEARD. HOW DID THAT EXPERIENCE MAKE YOU FEEL?

DATE:
_____

_____

_____

_____

_____

_____

_____

_____

_____

_____

_____

_____

_____

_____

_____

_____

_____

_____

_____

_____

The Seed: Reflecting on Who You Are

The Seed: Reflecting on Who You Are

EXPLORE YOUR RELATIONSHIP WITH VULNERABILITY. HOW DOES IT IMPACT YOUR ABILITY TO HEAL AND CONNECT WITH OTHERS?

DATE:

When is the last time you devoted quality time to yourself? Take yourself on a date. Be intentional about this time spent. Disconnect from everything and reconnect with yourself. Be mindful of your internal dialogue, sit with your emotions, and acknowledge the experience of being in your own presence.

DESCRIBE A SUPPORTIVE SPACE WHERE YOU FEEL SAFE TO SHARE YOUR STRUGGLES AND VICTORIES.

DATE: _____

_____
_____
_____
_____
_____
_____
_____
_____
_____
_____
_____
_____
_____
_____
_____
_____
_____
_____
_____
_____

The Seed: Reflecting on Who You Are

The Seed: Reflecting on Who You Are

REFLECT ON A TIME WHEN YOU FELT A SENSE OF BELONGING. HOW CAN YOU CREATE SPACES OF BELONGING FOR YOURSELF AND OTHERS?

DATE: _____

_____

_____

_____

_____

_____

_____

_____

_____

_____

_____

_____

_____

_____

_____

_____

_____

_____

_____

_____

_____

The Seed: Reflecting on Who You Are

WEEKLY CHECK-IN

THIS WEEK I'M GRATEFUL FOR

| 1 | 2 | 3 |

THINGS THAT MADE ME SMILE THIS WEEK

SOMETHING THAT
INSPIRED ME THIS WEEK

CONNECTIONS THAT I MADE THIS
WEEK

SOMETHING THAT
WORKED WELL THIS WEEK

AREA FOR IMPROVEMENT

Set your intention for the week

The Seed: Reflecting on Who You Are

DESCRIBE A ROLE OR RESPONSIBILITY YOU HOLD IN YOUR COMMUNITY OR FAMILY. HOW DOES IT CONTRIBUTE TO YOUR SENSE OF PURPOSE?

DATE:

The Seed: Reflecting on Who You Are

EXPLORE THE CONCEPT OF SELF-WORTH. HOW CAN YOU CULTIVATE A STRONG SENSE OF SELF-WORTH IN YOUR HEALING JOURNEY?

DATE: _____

The Seed: Reflecting on Who You Are

WHAT ARE THREE LIMITING BELIEFS THAT HOLD YOU BACK? HOW CAN YOU CHALLENGE AND OVERCOME THEM?

DATE:

The Seed: Reflecting on Who You Are

REFLECT ON A TIME WHEN YOU FELT A DEEP SENSE OF PURPOSE AND MEANING. WHAT CONTRIBUTED TO THAT FEELING?

DATE: _____

_____
_____
_____
_____
_____
_____
_____
_____
_____
_____
_____
_____
_____
_____
_____
_____
_____
_____
_____

The Seed: Reflecting on Who You Are

The Seed: Reflecting on Who You Are

WHAT ARE THE OUTWARD SIGNS YOU DISPLAY WHEN FEELING OVERWHELMED?

DATE:
_____

_____

_____

_____

_____

_____

_____

_____

_____

_____

_____

_____

_____

_____

_____

_____

_____

_____

The Seed: Reflecting on Who You Are

The Seed: Reflecting on Who You Are

WHAT DOES RESILIENCE MEAN TO YOU? HOW HAVE YOU DISPLAYED RESILIENCE IN YOUR LIFE THUS FAR?

DATE:
_____

_____
_____
_____
_____
_____
_____
_____
_____
_____
_____
_____
_____
_____
_____
_____
_____
_____
_____
_____
_____
_____
_____

The Seed: Reflecting on Who You Are

The Seed: Reflecting on Who You Are

"The way we think of ourselves has everything to do with how the world sees us and how we see ourselves successfully acknowledged by the world."
—Arlene Rankin

WEEKLY CHECK-IN

THIS WEEK I'M GRATEFUL FOR

| 1 | 2 | 3 |

THINGS THAT MADE ME SMILE THIS WEEK

SOMETHING THAT INSPIRED ME THIS WEEK

CONNECTIONS THAT I MADE THIS WEEK

SOMETHING THAT WORKED WELL THIS WEEK

AREA FOR IMPROVEMENT

Set your intention for the week

REFLECT ON THE RELATIONSHIP BETWEEN SPIRITUALITY AND YOUR HEALING JOURNEY. HOW DO THEY INTERSECT?

DATE:
_____

_____

_____

_____

_____

_____

_____

_____

_____

_____

_____

_____

_____

_____

_____

_____

_____

_____

_____

The Seed: Reflecting on Who You Are

The Seed: Reflecting on Who You Are

DESCRIBE A MOMENT WHEN YOUR INTUITION GUIDED YOU ON YOUR HEALING JOURNEY. HOW DO YOU TAP INTO AND TRUST YOUR INTUITION?

DATE: _____

The Seed: Reflecting on Who You Are

WHAT COPING MECHANISMS HAVE YOU DEVELOPED OVER TIME? WHICH ONES SERVE YOU, AND WHICH ONES NO LONGER DO?

DATE:
_____

_____
_____
_____
_____
_____
_____
_____
_____
_____
_____
_____
_____
_____
_____
_____
_____
_____
_____
_____
_____

The Seed: Reflecting on Who You Are

The Seed: Reflecting on Who You Are

WHAT MESSAGES—SPOKEN OR UNSPOKEN—DID YOU RECEIVE ABOUT PAIN AND RESILIENCE GROWING UP?

DATE: _____

_____
_____
_____
_____
_____
_____
_____
_____
_____
_____
_____
_____
_____
_____
_____
_____
_____
_____
_____
_____

The Seed: Reflecting on Who You Are

The Seed: Reflecting on Who You Are

DESCRIBE A SONG, POEM, OR PIECE OF ART THAT DEEPLY RESONATES WITH YOU. WHAT EMOTIONS DOES IT EVOKE? WHY?

DATE:

The Seed: Reflecting on Who You Are

EXPLORE THE CONCEPT OF SELF-FORGIVENESS. WHAT PAST MISTAKES OR REGRETS DO YOU NEED TO RELEASE IN ORDER TO HEAL?

DATE:

The Seed: Reflecting on Who You Are

WEEKLY CHECK-IN

THIS WEEK I'M GRATEFUL FOR

| 1 | 2 | 3 |

THINGS THAT MADE ME SMILE THIS WEEK

- _____
- _____
- _____

SOMETHING THAT INSPIRED ME THIS WEEK

CONNECTIONS THAT I MADE THIS WEEK

SOMETHING THAT WORKED WELL THIS WEEK

AREA FOR IMPROVEMENT

Set your intention for the week

The Seed: Reflecting on Who You Are

SECTION 2

BUDDING
CONSIDERING YOUR GROWTH REQUIREMENTS

Budding is described as the early stage of development that demonstrates the promise or potential of a plant. This is when a new organism is formed from the bud of an existing organism, or when you realize your potential.

Take a moment to think about how you currently nurture your soil or your soul. What are you literally and figuratively pouring into yourself? What are you watching? What are you listening to? Who is in your company? Who are you in conversation with? What are you pouring into yourself? Most seeds can't grow in darkness. Who and what are your sources of light? How frequently are you letting that light shine into the darkness? Practicing awareness of the things that you are feeding your seed impacts the overall growth of your garden.

EXPLORE YOUR RELATIONSHIP WITH SELF-CARE. WHAT ARE SOME WAYS YOU CAN PRIORITIZE YOUR WELL-BEING?

DATE:

Budding: Growth Requirements

Budding: Growth Requirements

WHAT ARE THREE SELF-CARE PRACTICES THAT NOURISH YOUR MIND, BODY, AND SOUL? HOW CAN YOU INCORPORATE THEM INTO YOUR ROUTINE?

DATE:
_____

_____
_____
_____
_____
_____
_____
_____
_____
_____
_____
_____
_____
_____
_____
_____
_____
_____
_____
_____
_____

Budding: Growth Requirements

Budding: Growth Requirements

HOW CAN YOU HONOR YOUR OWN HEALING WITHOUT FEELING LIKE YOU HAVE TO BE STRONG ALL THE TIME?

DATE:

Budding: Growth Requirements

Budding: Growth Requirements

WHAT DOES SELF-COMPASSION MEAN TO YOU? HOW CAN YOU PRACTICE IT MORE IN YOUR LIFE?

DATE:

Budding: Growth Requirements

Budding: Growth Requirements

WHAT ARE THREE AREAS OF YOUR LIFE WHERE YOU NEED TO PRACTICE MORE SELF-COMPASSION?

DATE:
_____

_____
_____
_____
_____
_____
_____
_____
_____
_____
_____
_____
_____
_____
_____
_____
_____
_____
_____
_____

Budding: Growth Requirements

Budding: Growth Requirements

HOW HAS SOCIETY'S PERCEPTION OF BLACK WOMEN (E.G., THE "STRONG BLACK WOMAN" TROPE) INFLUENCED THE WAY YOU HANDLE PAIN AND HEALING?   DATE:

Budding: Growth Requirements

Budding: Growth Requirements

WEEKLY CHECK-IN

THIS WEEK I'M GRATEFUL FOR

| 1 | 2 | 3 |

THINGS THAT MADE ME SMILE THIS WEEK

SOMETHING THAT
INSPIRED ME THIS WEEK

CONNECTIONS THAT I MADE THIS WEEK

SOMETHING THAT
WORKED WELL THIS WEEK

AREA FOR IMPROVEMENT

Set your intention for the week

Budding: Growth Requirements

EXPLORE YOUR RELATIONSHIP WITH ANGER.
HOW CAN YOU EXPRESS AND CHANNEL IT IN A
HEALTHY AND PRODUCTIVE WAY?

DATE:
_____

_____
_____
_____
_____
_____
_____
_____
_____
_____
_____
_____
_____
_____
_____
_____
_____
_____
_____
_____
_____

Budding: Growth Requirements

Budding: Growth Requirements

EXPLORE THE CONCEPT OF FORGIVENESS. WHO DO YOU NEED TO FORGIVE IN ORDER TO FIND HEALING AND LIBERATION?

DATE: _____

_____
_____
_____
_____
_____
_____
_____
_____
_____
_____
_____
_____
_____
_____
_____
_____
_____
_____

Budding: Growth Requirements

Budding: Growth Requirements

Self-love comprises four aspects: self-awareness, self-worth, self-esteem and self-care

Goal Setting

Identify the necessary steps to accomplish the desired change you aspire to achieve. While having goals is important, having a well-thought-out plan enhances the chances of attaining them. Consider a goal you want to reach and outline the actions required to move closer to achieving it.

Goal

Action Steps

1.

2.

3.

EXPLORE THE CONCEPT OF RADICAL SELF-LOVE. HOW CAN YOU PRACTICE RADICAL SELF-LOVE AND ACCEPTANCE ON YOUR HEALING JOURNEY?

DATE:
_____

_____
_____
_____
_____
_____
_____
_____
_____
_____
_____
_____
_____
_____
_____
_____
_____
_____
_____
_____
_____
_____

Budding: Growth Requirements

Budding: Growth Requirements

WHAT NARRATIVES ABOUT YOURSELF DO YOU WANT TO RELEASE?

DATE:

Budding: Growth Requirements

Budding: Growth Requirements

LIST FIVE THINGS THAT BRING YOU JOY AND MAKE YOU FEEL ALIVE. HOW CAN YOU PRIORITIZE INCORPORATING THEM INTO YOUR LIFE?

DATE:

Budding: Growth Requirements

Budding: Growth Requirements

HOW DO YOU DEFINE SUCCESS AND FULFILLMENT? DOES YOUR DEFINITION ALIGN WITH SOCIETAL EXPECTATIONS?

DATE:
_____

_____
_____
_____
_____
_____
_____
_____
_____
_____
_____
_____
_____
_____
_____
_____
_____
_____
_____
_____
_____
_____
_____

Budding: Growth Requirements

Budding: Growth Requirements

WEEKLY CHECK-IN

THIS WEEK I'M GRATEFUL FOR

| 1 | 2 | 3 |

THINGS THAT MADE ME SMILE THIS WEEK

☺ _____
☺ _____
☺ _____

SOMETHING THAT
INSPIRED ME THIS WEEK

CONNECTIONS THAT I MADE THIS WEEK

SOMETHING THAT
WORKED WELL THIS WEEK

AREA FOR IMPROVEMENT

Set your intention for the week

Budding: Growth Requirements

WHAT ADVICE WOULD YOU GIVE TO A YOUNGER WOMAN OF COLOR WHO IS EMBARKING ON HER HEALING JOURNEY?

DATE:

Budding: Growth Requirements

Budding: Growth Requirements

SECTION 3

SPROUTING

OVERCOMING CHALLENGES

Sprouts possess exceptional qualities. They can flourish in various climates throughout the year, without relying on soil or sunlight, while remaining rich in vital vitamins and minerals. Cultivated without chemical sprays, they grow and multiply quickly, providing the essential nutrients for rooting and future flowering.

Just like sprouts pushing through the soil to reach the sunlight, we too continue to grow and evolve despite the challenges and difficulties we face along the way. These obstacles may initially seem overwhelming, but they ultimately serve as opportunities for us to learn, adapt, and become stronger individuals. Like a resilient plant that perseveres through harsh conditions, we too can thrive and reach our full potential even in the face of adversity. Our growth knows no bounds, and with each challenge we overcome, we become more capable and resilient in navigating the journey of life.

WHAT ARE THREE SELF-LIMITING BELIEFS THAT NO LONGER SERVE YOU? HOW CAN YOU REFRAME THEM INTO EMPOWERING BELIEFS?

DATE:

Sprouting: Overcoming Challenges

Sprouting: Overcoming Challenges

WHAT ARE THREE FEARS THAT PREVENT YOU FROM FULLY EMBRACING YOUR HEALING JOURNEY? HOW CAN YOU OVERCOME THEM?

DATE:
_____

_____

_____

_____

_____

_____

_____

_____

_____

_____

_____

_____

_____

_____

_____

_____

_____

_____

Sprouting: Overcoming Challenges

Sprouting: Overcoming Challenges

REFLECT ON A TIME WHEN YOU OVERCAME SELF-DOUBT OR INSECURITIES. HOW DID THAT EXPERIENCE IMPACT YOUR HEALING?

DATE:
_____

_____
_____
_____
_____
_____
_____
_____
_____
_____
_____
_____
_____
_____
_____
_____
_____
_____
_____
_____

Sprouting: Overcoming Challenges

Sprouting: Overcoming Challenges

REFLECT ON A TIME WHEN YOU FACED A FEAR HEAD-ON. HOW DID THAT EXPERIENCE IMPACT YOUR HEALING JOURNEY?

DATE:
_____

_____
_____
_____
_____
_____
_____
_____
_____
_____
_____
_____
_____
_____
_____
_____
_____
_____
_____

Sprouting: Overcoming Challenges

Sprouting: Overcoming Challenges

EXPLORE YOUR RELATIONSHIP WITH BODY IMAGE. WHAT SOCIETAL PRESSURES OR EXPECTATIONS DO YOU NEED TO RELEASE?

DATE:

Sprouting: Overcoming Challenges

Sprouting: Overcoming Challenges

WEEKLY CHECK-IN

THIS WEEK I'M GRATEFUL FOR

| 1 | 2 | 3 |

THINGS THAT MADE ME SMILE THIS WEEK

SOMETHING THAT
INSPIRED ME THIS WEEK

CONNECTIONS THAT I MADE THIS WEEK

SOMETHING THAT
WORKED WELL THIS WEEK

AREA FOR IMPROVEMENT

Set your intention for the week

Sprouting: Overcoming Challenges

REFLECT ON A TIME WHEN YOU CONFRONTED INTERNALIZED RACISM OR NEGATIVE SOCIETAL MESSAGES. HOW DID YOU CHALLENGE AND OVERCOME THEM?

DATE:

Sprouting: Overcoming Challenges

Sprouting: Overcoming Challenges

EXPLORE THE INFLUENCE OF CULTURAL STEREOTYPES ON YOUR SELF-PERCEPTION AND HOW YOU CAN CHALLENGE THEM.

DATE:
_____

_____
_____
_____
_____
_____
_____
_____
_____
_____
_____
_____
_____
_____
_____
_____
_____
_____
_____
_____
_____

Sprouting: Overcoming Challenges

Sprouting: Overcoming Challenges

REFLECT ON A TIME WHEN YOU EXPERIENCED RACIAL TRAUMA OR WITNESSED RACIAL INJUSTICE. HOW DID IT IMPACT YOUR MENTAL HEALTH AND HEALING? DATE:

Sprouting: Overcoming Challenges

Sprouting: Overcoming Challenges

HOW DO YOU NAVIGATE AND MANAGE MICROAGGRESSIONS OR RACIAL BIAS IN YOUR DAILY LIFE?

DATE:

Sprouting: Overcoming Challenges

Sprouting: Overcoming Challenges

DESCRIBE A TIME WHEN YOU WERE RESILIENT IN THE FACE OF INJUSTICE. HOW DID THAT EXPERIENCE SHAPE YOUR HEALING JOURNEY?

DATE: _____

_____
_____
_____
_____
_____
_____
_____
_____
_____
_____
_____
_____
_____
_____
_____
_____
_____
_____

Sprouting: Overcoming Challenges

Steps to CULTIVATE RESILIENCE

✓ Develop a Strong Support System: Surround yourself with positive influences.

✓ Practice Self-Care: Activities like meditation, reading, or even walking can rejuvenate your mind.

✓ Embrace Change: Accept that change is a part of life and look for ways to adapt and learn.

✓ Set Realistic Goals: Setting and working toward achievable goals can boost your confidence and sense of purpose.

Action Plan:
Choose one area where you feel least resilient and actively work on it for a month. Note your progress and obstacles, and refine your approach as needed.

REFLECT ON A TIME WHEN YOU FELT MARGINALIZED. HOW DID YOU FIND STRENGTH AND RESILIENCE IN THAT EXPERIENCE?

DATE:
_____

_____
_____
_____
_____
_____
_____
_____
_____
_____
_____
_____
_____
_____
_____
_____
_____
_____
_____
_____
_____

Sprouting: Overcoming Challenges

Sprouting: Overcoming Challenges

WEEKLY CHECK-IN

THIS WEEK I'M GRATEFUL FOR

1.

2.

3.

THINGS THAT MADE ME SMILE THIS WEEK

☺ ___
☺ ___
☺ ___

SOMETHING THAT INSPIRED ME THIS WEEK

CONNECTIONS THAT I MADE THIS WEEK

SOMETHING THAT WORKED WELL THIS WEEK

AREA FOR IMPROVEMENT

Set your intention for the week

Sprouting: Overcoming Challenges

DESCRIBE A TIME WHEN YOU HAD TO ADVOCATE FOR YOURSELF OR OTHERS.

DATE:
_____

_____
_____
_____
_____
_____
_____
_____
_____
_____
_____
_____
_____
_____
_____
_____
_____
_____
_____
_____
_____

Sprouting: Overcoming Challenges

Sprouting: Overcoming Challenges

REFLECT ON A TIME WHEN YOU FELT AS IF YOU WERE NOT ENOUGH. HOW CAN YOU REFRAME THAT NARRATIVE AND CULTIVATE SELF-ACCEPTANCE?

DATE:
_____

_____
_____
_____
_____
_____
_____
_____
_____
_____
_____
_____
_____
_____
_____
_____
_____
_____
_____

Sprouting: Overcoming Challenges

Sprouting: Overcoming Challenges

EXPLORE YOUR EXPERIENCE OF IMPOSTER SYNDROME. HOW DOES IT IMPACT YOUR SELF-ESTEEM AND CONFIDENCE?

DATE:

Sprouting: Overcoming Challenges

Sprouting: Overcoming Challenges

REFLECT ON A TIME WHEN YOU HAD TO MAKE A DIFFICULT DECISION FOR YOUR OWN WELL-BEING. HOW DID THAT CHOICE CONTRIBUTE TO YOUR HEALING?

DATE:
_____

_____
_____
_____
_____
_____
_____
_____
_____
_____
_____
_____
_____
_____
_____
_____
_____
_____
_____
_____
_____
_____

Sprouting: Overcoming Challenges

Sprouting: Overcoming Challenges

REFLECT ON A TIME WHEN YOU HAD TO SET BOUNDARIES TO PROTECT YOUR MENTAL HEALTH AND WELL-BEING.

DATE:

Sprouting: Overcoming Challenges

Sprouting: Overcoming Challenges

WHAT HURTS? WHY DOES IT HURT? HOW DO YOU WANT TO FEEL?

DATE:

Sprouting: Overcoming Challenges

Sprouting: Overcoming Challenges

WEEKLY CHECK-IN

THIS WEEK I'M GRATEFUL FOR

| 1 | 2 | 3 |

THINGS THAT MADE ME SMILE THIS WEEK

SOMETHING THAT INSPIRED ME THIS WEEK

CONNECTIONS THAT I MADE THIS WEEK

SOMETHING THAT WORKED WELL THIS WEEK

AREA FOR IMPROVEMENT

Set your intention for the week

REFLECT ON A TIME WHEN YOU WERE ABLE TO FORGIVE SOMEONE WHO HAD HURT YOU DEEPLY. HOW DID THAT ACT OF FORGIVENESS IMPACT YOUR HEALING?

DATE:

Sprouting: Overcoming Challenges

Sprouting: Overcoming Challenges

WRITE A LETTER OF FORGIVENESS TO SOMEONE WHO HAS CAUSED YOU PAIN OR HARM. CAN YOU FIND COMPASSION IN YOUR HEART FOR THEM?

DATE:
_____

_____
_____
_____
_____
_____
_____
_____
_____
_____
_____
_____
_____
_____
_____
_____
_____
_____
_____
_____
_____
_____
_____
_____
_____

Sprouting: Overcoming Challenges

Sprouting: Overcoming Challenges

DESCRIBE A MOMENT OF TRIUMPH OR RESILIENCE IN YOUR LIFE. HOW DID YOU OVERCOME THE CHALLENGES?

DATE:
_____

_____
_____
_____
_____
_____
_____
_____
_____
_____
_____
_____
_____
_____
_____
_____
_____
_____
_____

Sprouting: Overcoming Challenges

Sprouting: Overcoming Challenges

BOX BREATHING

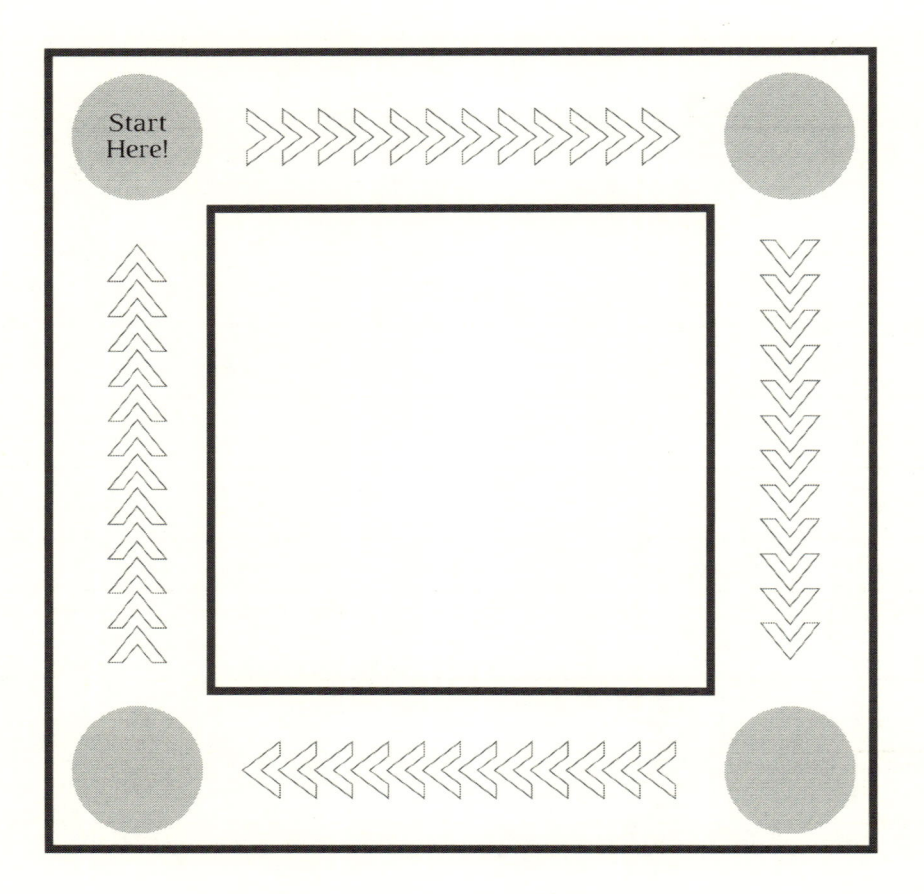

Place your finger on the dot that says "Start Here!"
Take a deep breath in and count to 4.
Move your finger to the next dot as you release your breath.
Breathe in at each corner and count to 4 until you complete the box.

Sprouting: Overcoming Challenges

DESCRIBE A SACRED SPACE OR A QUIET CORNER IN YOUR HOME WHERE YOU CAN RETREAT AND FIND SOLACE.

DATE:

Sprouting: Overcoming Challenges

Sprouting: Overcoming Challenges

SECTION 4
FLOWERING
BEARING FLOWERS AND FRUIT

Flowering is a significant stage in the plant life cycle. During this time, plants produce flowers as part of their reproductive process. This stage signifies the optimal development of the plant, marking the transition to the reproductive phase. Flowers play a crucial role in attracting pollinators, such as bees and butterflies, to facilitate the process of fertilization and seed production. The beauty and diversity of flowers also contribute to the overall aesthetics of nature, making flowering a remarkable and essential phenomenon in the natural world.

Like plants, humans also have the capacity to bloom and grow. Just as a plant starts as a seed and transforms into a beautiful flower, we go through various stages of development and change throughout our lives. We experience moments of growth, where we learn new things, develop new skills, and become better versions of ourselves. Each of us has the potential to bloom and flourish, just like a plant reaching towards the sun to soak in its warmth and light. It is a reminder that growth and transformation are natural processes that we all go through, much like the cycles of nature.

WRITE A LOVE LETTER TO YOUR INNER CHILD, ACKNOWLEDGING HER STRENGTH AND RESILIENCE.

DATE:

Flowering: Bearing Flowers and Fruit

Flowering: Bearing Flowers and Fruit

LIST FIVE THINGS YOU ARE GENUINELY PROUD OF ACCOMPLISHING IN YOUR LIFE. CELEBRATE YOUR ACHIEVEMENTS.

DATE:

Flowering: Bearing Flowers and Fruit

Flowering: Bearing Flowers and Fruit

WEEKLY CHECK-IN

THIS WEEK I'M GRATEFUL FOR

| 1 | 2 | 3 |

THINGS THAT MADE ME SMILE THIS WEEK

SOMETHING THAT INSPIRED ME THIS WEEK

CONNECTIONS THAT I MADE THIS WEEK

SOMETHING THAT WORKED WELL THIS WEEK

AREA FOR IMPROVEMENT

Set your intention for the week

Flowering: Bearing Flowers and Fruit

REFLECT ON A TIME WHEN YOU FELT A DEEP SENSE OF PEACE AND CALM. WHAT CONTRIBUTED TO THAT FEELING?

DATE:

Flowering: Bearing Flowers and Fruit

Flowering: Bearing Flowers and Fruit

WHAT PARTS OF YOURSELF ARE YOU READY TO EMBRACE THAT YOU MAY HAVE ONCE SUPPRESSED?

DATE: _____

_____
_____
_____
_____
_____
_____
_____
_____
_____
_____
_____
_____
_____
_____
_____
_____
_____
_____
_____
_____

Flowering: Bearing Flowers and Fruit

Flowering: Bearing Flowers and Fruit

WHAT ROLE DOES GRATITUDE PLAY IN YOUR HEALING JOURNEY? LIST TEN THINGS YOU ARE GRATEFUL FOR TODAY.

DATE:

Flowering: Bearing Flowers and Fruit

A moment of GRATITUDE

things:

people:

words:

events:

I am Grateful for

habits:

activities:

DESCRIBE A MOMENT WHEN YOU FELT CONNECTED TO A VIBRANT AND SUPPORTIVE COMMUNITY OF WOMEN OF COLOR. HOW DID IT MAKE YOU FEEL?

DATE:

Flowering: Bearing Flowers and Fruit

Flowering: Bearing Flowers and Fruit

WHAT IS A MOMENT WHEN YOU FELT A SENSE OF GRATITUDE FOR THE SUPPORT OF YOUR COMMUNITY. HOW DID THAT EXPERIENCE IMPACT YOUR PERSPECTIVE ON SISTERHOOD?

DATE:

Flowering: Bearing Flowers and Fruit

Flowering: Bearing Flowers and Fruit

IF YOU COULD REWRITE YOUR STORY, WHAT WOULD HEALING AND WHOLENESS LOOK LIKE FOR YOU?

DATE:

Flowering: Bearing Flowers and Fruit

Flowering: Bearing Flowers and Fruit

WEEKLY CHECK-IN

THIS WEEK I'M GRATEFUL FOR

| 1 | 2 | 3 |

THINGS THAT MADE ME SMILE THIS WEEK

SOMETHING THAT INSPIRED ME THIS WEEK

CONNECTIONS THAT I MADE THIS WEEK

SOMETHING THAT WORKED WELL THIS WEEK

AREA FOR IMPROVEMENT

Set your intention for the week

Flowering: Bearing Flowers and Fruit

WRITE A LETTER TO A WOMAN OF COLOR WHO HAS INSPIRED YOU, EXPRESSING YOUR GRATITUDE AND ADMIRATION.

DATE: _____

_____
_____
_____
_____
_____
_____
_____
_____
_____
_____
_____
_____
_____
_____
_____
_____
_____
_____

Flowering: Bearing Flowers and Fruit

Flowering: Bearing Flowers and Fruit

WHO ARE YOU OUTSIDE OF YOUR TRAUMA?

DATE:

Flowering: Bearing Flowers and Fruit

Flowering: Bearing Flowers and Fruit

DESCRIBE A MENTOR OR ROLE MODEL WHO HAS INSPIRED YOU ON YOUR HEALING JOURNEY. WHAT QUALITIES DO THEY POSSESS?

DATE:

Flowering: Bearing Flowers and Fruit

Flowering: Bearing Flowers and Fruit

DESCRIBE A MOMENT OF PROFOUND GRATITUDE IN YOUR LIFE. HOW DID IT SHAPE YOUR HEALING JOURNEY?

DATE:
_____

_____
_____
_____
_____
_____
_____
_____
_____
_____
_____
_____
_____
_____
_____
_____
_____
_____
_____
_____
_____

Flowering: Bearing Flowers and Fruit

Flowering: Bearing Flowers and Fruit

WHAT BOUNDARIES DO YOU NEED TO SET TO PROTECT YOUR PEACE AND WELL-BEING?

DATE:
_____

_____
_____
_____
_____
_____
_____
_____
_____
_____
_____
_____
_____
_____
_____
_____
_____
_____
_____

Flowering: Bearing Flowers and Fruit

Flowering: Bearing Flowers and Fruit

WRITE A LETTER OF GRATITUDE TO YOUR BODY. WHAT IS SOMETHING YOU APPRECIATE ABOUT YOUR PHYSICAL SELF?

DATE:

___

Flowering: Bearing Flowers and Fruit

Flowering: Bearing Flowers and Fruit

WEEKLY CHECK-IN

THIS WEEK I'M GRATEFUL FOR

| 1 | 2 | 3 |

THINGS THAT MADE ME SMILE THIS WEEK

SOMETHING THAT
INSPIRED ME THIS WEEK

CONNECTIONS THAT I MADE THIS WEEK

SOMETHING THAT
WORKED WELL THIS WEEK

AREA FOR IMPROVEMENT

Set your intention for the week

Flowering: Bearing Flowers and Fruit

WHAT DOES HEALING MEAN TO YOU, AND HOW WILL YOU KNOW WHEN YOU'RE LIVING IN IT?

DATE:

Flowering: Bearing Flowers and Fruit

Flowering: Bearing Flowers and Fruit

WHAT DOES SELF-LOVE AND SELF-ACCEPTANCE LOOK LIKE FOR YOU IN THIS SEASON OF YOUR LIFE?

DATE:

_____
_____
_____
_____
_____
_____
_____
_____
_____
_____
_____
_____
_____
_____
_____
_____
_____
_____
_____
_____
_____
_____
_____

Flowering: Bearing Flowers and Fruit

Flowering: Bearing Flowers and Fruit

SECTION 5
GROUNDING
ACKNOWLEDGING YOUR ROOTS

Acknowledging your roots and celebrating their influence is a powerful way to honor where you come from and the people who have shaped you. By recognizing the traditions, values, and experiences passed down to you, you can gain a deeper understanding of your identity and connections to your heritage. Embracing the influences of your roots can provide a sense of belonging and pride, as well as a source of inspiration for your journey ahead. Whether through cultural practices, family stories, or ancestral teachings, celebrating your roots can enrich your life and help you appreciate the unique tapestry of your origins.

HOW HAS YOUR CULTURAL HERITAGE PLAYED A ROLE IN SHAPING YOUR IDENTITY AND HEALING JOURNEY?

DATE:

Grounding: Acknowledging Your Roots

Grounding: Acknowledging Your Roots

DESCRIBE THE WAYS IN WHICH YOUR CULTURAL IDENTITY INTERSECTS WITH YOUR MENTAL HEALTH JOURNEY.

DATE:
_____

_____
_____
_____
_____
_____
_____
_____
_____
_____
_____
_____
_____
_____
_____
_____
_____
_____
_____
_____
_____
_____

Grounding: Acknowledging Your Roots

Grounding: Acknowledging Your Roots

REFLECT ON A TIME WHEN YOU FELT A DEEP CONNECTION TO YOUR ANCESTRAL ROOTS. WHAT WISDOM OR GUIDANCE DOES IT OFFER ON YOUR JOURNEY?

DATE:
_____

_____
_____
_____
_____
_____
_____
_____
_____
_____
_____
_____
_____
_____
_____
_____
_____
_____
_____
_____
_____

Grounding: Acknowledging Your Roots

Grounding: Acknowledging Your Roots

DESCRIBE A RITUAL OR PRACTICE THAT BRINGS YOU A SENSE OF SPIRITUAL CONNECTION AND RENEWAL.

DATE: _____

_____
_____
_____
_____
_____
_____
_____
_____
_____
_____
_____
_____
_____
_____
_____
_____
_____
_____
_____

Grounding: Acknowledging Your Roots

Grounding: Acknowledging Your Roots

WEEKLY CHECK-IN

THIS WEEK I'M GRATEFUL FOR

| 1 | 2 | 3 |

THINGS THAT MADE ME SMILE THIS WEEK

- _____
- _____
- _____

SOMETHING THAT INSPIRED ME THIS WEEK

CONNECTIONS THAT I MADE THIS WEEK

SOMETHING THAT WORKED WELL THIS WEEK

AREA FOR IMPROVEMENT

Set your intention for the week
_____
_____
_____

Grounding: Acknowledging Your Roots

WHAT ARE SOME CULTURAL OR ANCESTRAL HEALING PRACTICES THAT RESONATE WITH YOU? HOW CAN YOU INCORPORATE THEM INTO YOUR LIFE?

DATE:

___

Grounding: Acknowledging Your Roots

Grounding: Acknowledging Your Roots

REFLECT ON THE POWER OF STORYTELLING AND ITS ROLE IN YOUR JOURNEY. HOW CAN YOU HARNESS THE POWER OF YOUR OWN NARRATIVE?

DATE:
_____

_____
_____
_____
_____
_____
_____
_____
_____
_____
_____
_____
_____
_____
_____
_____
_____
_____
_____
_____
_____
_____
_____
_____
_____

Grounding: Acknowledging Your Roots

Grounding: Acknowledging Your Roots

WRITE A LETTER TO YOUR ANCESTORS, EXPRESSING GRATITUDE FOR THEIR RESILIENCE AND STRENGTH. HOW DO YOU CARRY THEIR LEGACY?

DATE:
_____

_____
_____
_____
_____
_____
_____
_____
_____
_____
_____
_____
_____
_____
_____
_____
_____
_____
_____
_____
_____

Grounding: Acknowledging Your Roots

Grounding: Acknowledging Your Roots

WRITE A LOVE LETTER TO YOUR CULTURAL HERITAGE, EMBRACING AND CELEBRATING ITS RICHNESS AND BEAUTY.

DATE:

Grounding: Acknowledging Your Roots

Grounding: Acknowledging Your Roots

WHAT DOES HEALING MEAN TO YOU, AND HOW WILL YOU KNOW WHEN YOU'RE LIVING IN IT?

DATE:
_____

_____
_____
_____
_____
_____
_____
_____
_____
_____
_____
_____
_____
_____
_____
_____
_____
_____
_____
_____
_____
_____
_____

Grounding: Acknowledging Your Roots

Grounding: Acknowledging Your Roots

REFLECT ON A TIME WHEN YOU FELT A SPIRITUAL OR ANCESTRAL PRESENCE GUIDING YOUR HEALING JOURNEY.

DATE:
_____

_____
_____
_____
_____
_____
_____
_____
_____
_____
_____
_____
_____
_____
_____
_____
_____
_____
_____
_____
_____
_____
_____

Grounding: Acknowledging Your Roots

Grounding: Acknowledging Your Roots

WEEKLY CHECK-IN

THIS WEEK I'M GRATEFUL FOR

| 1 | 2 | 3 |

THINGS THAT MADE ME SMILE THIS WEEK

SOMETHING THAT INSPIRED ME THIS WEEK

CONNECTIONS THAT I MADE THIS WEEK

SOMETHING THAT WORKED WELL THIS WEEK

AREA FOR IMPROVEMENT

Set your intention for the week

Grounding: Acknowledging Your Roots

WHAT ARE SOME CULTURAL TRADITIONS OR CEREMONIES YOU CAN CREATE TO HONOR YOUR HEALING JOURNEY?

DATE:
_____

_____
_____
_____
_____
_____
_____
_____
_____
_____
_____
_____
_____
_____
_____
_____
_____
_____
_____
_____
_____
_____
_____
_____

Grounding: Acknowledging Your Roots

Grounding: Acknowledging Your Roots

REFLECT ON THE IMPACT OF GENERATIONAL TRAUMA ON YOUR JOURNEY. HOW CAN YOU BREAK THE CYCLE OF INTERGENERATIONAL PAIN?

DATE:

___

Grounding: Acknowledging Your Roots

Grounding: Acknowledging Your Roots

DESCRIBE A TIME WHEN YOU FELT TRULY SUPPORTED BY YOUR CHOSEN FAMILY OR FRIENDS. HOW DID THEIR SUPPORT CONTRIBUTE TO YOUR HEALING?

DATE:

_____
_____
_____
_____
_____
_____
_____
_____
_____
_____
_____
_____
_____
_____
_____
_____
_____
_____

Grounding: Acknowledging Your Roots

Grounding: Acknowledging Your Roots

REFLECT ON A TIME WHEN YOU FELT A DEEP SENSE OF CONNECTION AND SISTERHOOD WITH OTHER WOMEN OF COLOR. HOW DID IT SHAPE YOU?

DATE:

_____

_____
_____
_____
_____
_____
_____
_____
_____
_____
_____
_____
_____
_____
_____
_____
_____
_____
_____
_____

Grounding: Acknowledging Your Roots

Grounding: Acknowledging Your Roots

WRITE A LETTER TO A WOMAN OF COLOR WHO HAS SUPPORTED YOU ON YOUR HEALING JOURNEY, EXPRESSING YOUR HEARTFELT GRATITUDE.

DATE:
_____

_____
_____
_____
_____
_____
_____
_____
_____
_____
_____
_____
_____
_____
_____
_____
_____
_____
_____
_____
_____
_____
_____
_____

Grounding: Acknowledging Your Roots

Grounding: Acknowledging Your Roots

EXPLORE THE CONCEPT OF INTERCONNECTED HEALING. HOW DO YOUR PERSONAL HEALING AND GROWTH IMPACT THE COLLECTIVE HEALING OF WOMEN OF COLOR?

DATE:

Grounding: Acknowledging Your Roots

Grounding: Acknowledging Your Roots

WRITE A LETTER TO YOUR PAST SELF, FORGIVING YOURSELF FOR YOUR PAST.

DATE: _____

_____
_____
_____
_____
_____
_____
_____
_____
_____
_____
_____
_____
_____
_____
_____
_____
_____
_____
_____

Grounding: Acknowledging Your Roots

Grounding: Acknowledging Your Roots

SECTION 6
GRATITUDE
ADMIRING YOUR GARDEN

Practicing gratitude has far reaching effects. Studies have shown that practicing gratitude can help to improve our overall mental health, foster healthier relationship with the self as well as our interpersonal relationships, and better one's physical healthy as well.

Living your life with gratitude helps you notice the little wins and take joy even in the mundane. These small moments come together to create a web of well-being that, over time, strengthens your ability to recognize and celebrate the good.

You've done the work. Take some time to practice gratitude.

HARNESSING THE POWER OF

Positive Affirmations

Positive affirmations are short, powerful statements that help you to control your thoughts, overcome negative patterns, and reinforce a belief in yourself.

Why Affirmations Matter:

- ✓ **Rewire Thought Patterns:** With repetition, they can change the neural pathways in your brain.

- ✓ **Counteract Negativity:** They're a tool to fight back against self-doubt and fear.

- ✓ **Fuel Growth:** Affirmations can serve as reminders of your capability and potential.

Crafting Your
PERSONAL AFFIRMATIONS:

✓ Stay Positive: Frame affirmations in a positive manner, focusing on what you want, not what you want to avoid.

✓ Present Tense: Phrase them as if they're happening now — "I am" instead of "I will be."

✓ Believable: They should resonate with you, even if they stretch your current beliefs.

Exercise:

Write down three affirmations tailored to your personal aspirations or challenges that empower and uplift you. Repeat them every morning for a week.

1.

2.

3.

WEEKLY CHECK-IN

THIS WEEK I'M GRATEFUL FOR

| 1 | 2 | 3 |

THINGS THAT MADE ME SMILE THIS WEEK

SOMETHING THAT INSPIRED ME THIS WEEK

CONNECTIONS THAT I MADE THIS WEEK

SOMETHING THAT WORKED WELL THIS WEEK

AREA FOR IMPROVEMENT

Set your intention for the week

Gratitude: Admiring Your Garden

DESCRIBE A MANTRA OR AN AFFIRMATION THAT GROUNDS AND SUPPORTS YOU ON YOUR HEALING JOURNEY.

DATE:

Gratitude: Admiring Your Garden

Gratitude: Admiring Your Garden

DESCRIBE A TIME WHEN YOU FELT IMMENSE JOY AND CONTENTMENT. WHAT CONTRIBUTED TO THAT FEELING?

DATE:

Gratitude: Admiring Your Garden

Gratitude: Admiring Your Garden

REFLECT ON A TIME WHEN YOU FELT A SENSE OF LIBERATION AND FREEDOM. WHAT CONTRIBUTED TO THAT FEELING?

DATE:

Gratitude: Admiring Your Garden

Gratitude: Admiring Your Garden

REFLECT ON YOUR DREAMS AND ASPIRATIONS.
WHAT STEPS CAN YOU TAKE TO MANIFEST THEM
IN YOUR LIFE?   DATE:
_____

_____
_____
_____
_____
_____
_____
_____
_____
_____
_____
_____
_____
_____
_____
_____
_____
_____
_____
_____
_____
_____

Gratitude: Admiring Your Garden

Gratitude: Admiring Your Garden

WRITE A LETTER TO YOUR FUTURE SELF, DETAILING THE HOPES AND DREAMS YOU HAVE FOR YOUR HEALING JOURNEY.

DATE: _____

_____
_____
_____
_____
_____
_____
_____
_____
_____
_____
_____
_____
_____
_____
_____
_____
_____
_____
_____
_____
_____
_____

Gratitude: Admiring Your Garden

Gratitude: Admiring Your Garden

HOW CAN YOU CELEBRATE YOURSELF AND YOUR PROGRESS, NO MATTER HOW SMALL?

DATE:

Gratitude: Admiring Your Garden

Gratitude: Admiring Your Garden

5 - 4 - 3 - 2 - 1
Grounding Technique

A calming technique that connects you with the present by exploring the five senses.
Instructions: Sitting or standing, take a deep breath in, and complete the following questions.

5 — 5 things you can see

4 — 4 things you can touch

3 — 3 things you can hear

2 — 2 things you can smell

1 — 1 thing you can taste

WRITE A LETTER TO YOUR FUTURE SELF, ENVISIONING THE HEALED AND EMPOWERED WOMAN YOU ASPIRE TO BECOME.

DATE:

Gratitude: Admiring Your Garden

Gratitude: Admiring Your Garden

ENVISION YOUR FUTURE SELF. ATTACH IMAGES BELOW THAT ALIGN WITH YOUR GOALS FOR YOURSELF AND YOUR HEALING JOURNEY.

Gratitude: Admiring Your Garden

I'm so proud of you!